THE HEYDAY OF STEWARTS LANE
AND ITS LOCOMOTIVES

R. C. RILEY

Ian Allan PUBLISHING

Dedicated to Richard Hardy
Shedmaster 1952-5
who would not have tolerated
untidiness in the yard.

Front cover: Specially-groomed 'West Country' class 4-6-2 No 34091 *Weymouth* stands at Stewarts Lane shed on 27 October 1957 in readiness to work the down 'Golden Arrow'. On this occasion both the 'Britannia' 4-6-2s normally used were stopped for repairs; they left the SR in June 1958. *R. C. Riley*

Back cover: On the last day of steam on the Chatham line to the Kent Coast, Sunday 14 June 1959, 'King Arthur' class 4-6-0 No 30804 *Sir Cador of Cornwall* approaches Bromley South with an up empty-stock train. The branch line from Copyhold Junction (Haywards Heath) to Horsted Keynes had been singled so that one line could accommodate the new electric multiple-units; now, it would store the displaced Mausell steam stock awaiting scrap. *R. C. Riley*

Title page: The 'Night Ferry' service between London Victoria and Paris Gare du Nord, via Dover and Dunkirk, was inaugurated in 1936. It brought the unfamiliar sight of blue Wagons Lits sleeping cars to SR lines. Carrying the headboard on 15 September 1957 was the first (and appropriately-named) Bulleid Pacific No 35001 *Channel Packet*. The service lasted exactly 44 years, being withdrawn in October 1980. *R. C. Riley*

Left: 'Britannia' class 4-6-2 No 70014 *Iron Duke*, cleaned in readiness to work the down 'Golden Arrow'. This train was introduced in 1929, at that time with First-class Pullman cars only, and received a headboard only when it was reintroduced after the war in 1946. The flags, incidentally, were changed daily! *R. C. Riley*

First published 2001

ISBN 0 7110 2791 9

Published by Ian Allan Publishing

an imprint of Ian Allan Publishing Ltd, Hersham, Surrey KT12 4RG.
Printed by Ian Allan Printing Ltd, Hersham, Surrey KT12 4RG.

Code: 0105/B3

Introduction

For many years Stewarts Lane shed had one of the largest allocations of any shed on the Southern Railway. It had its origins in 1862 when the London Chatham & Dover Railway was completing its Metropolitan Extension to Victoria and later to Ludgate Hill. The LCDR purchased the 68-acre site of Longhedge Farm for the construction of its running shed together with the locomotive and carriage works. Very wisely, the company allowed for expansion, and this was soon needed when the original crescent-shaped shed, with all roads leading to a turntable, was rebuilt in 1881. The new shed had 16 roads and it was this building which survived into BR days.

At first the LCDR main line to Victoria took the low-level line at Factory Junction and passed the throat of the Longhedge shed. In 1863 a station was provided here and named 'Stewarts Lane'. Unsatisfactory operation over this line prompted the LCDR to build the present high-level line on the viaduct. This opened at the beginning of 1867, and, with Battersea Park and Wandsworth Road stations being close at hand, the short life of Stewarts Lane station came to an end. It was to be nearly 60 years before the name appeared again.

The LCDR locomotive and carriage works were very well equipped and highly regarded by the technical press of the day. The locomotive erecting shop turned out 54 new locomotives between 1869 and 1904. The two companies serving Kent, the LCDR and the South Eastern Railway (SER), had been in bitter competition for many years, but this came to an end in 1899 when both came under the care of the South Eastern & Chatham Railway (SECR) Managing Committee, although continuing to exist as separate companies. As a result, new locomotive construction was transferred to the extended former SER works at Ashford. Nevertheless, the erecting shop at Longhedge continued to carry out intermediate repairs on 'D1'/'E1' 4-4-0s, 'C' 0-6-0s and tank engines until the 1950s.

Prior to World War 1 all continental services used Charing Cross, but the restricted layout caused them to be transferred to Victoria in 1920. Since weight limits on the former LCDR line restricted the locomotives permitted to traverse it to the 'D' and 'E' class 4-4-0s this brought about the very successful rebuilding of some of these engines. The 'D1' and 'E1' class engines then handled all the continental boat train traffic until the line was passed for heavier engines.

When the Civil Engineers had started their upgrading work on the line, the first 10 of the newly-constructed 'King Arthur' class 4-6-0s (Nos 763-72) were allocated to the depot in 1925. Built by the North British Locomotive Co, Glasgow, these engines were known as the 'Scotch Arthurs'. Initially they were confined to the Tonbridge route, and trains on the Chatham line or via Maidstone East continued to be worked by the rebuilt 4-4-0s. By 1927 these two routes became available to the 4-6-0s. The 'King Arthurs' could haul a 425-ton load, compared with the 300-ton allowance for the 4-4-0s, although these regularly double-headed heavier trains.

The appearance of the powerful 'Lord Nelson' class 4-6-0s at the shed in 1928 again increased the loads of the continental expresses. They were permitted to haul 480 tons made up of 10 coaches, two Pullman cars and two vans. The usual allowance of 90 minutes for the 78 miles between Victoria and Dover Marine does not look impressive, but on this route, with its severe curves and adverse gradients, it required a high standard of enginemanship.

The London, Brighton & South Coast Railway (LBSCR), joint user of Victoria station, had its roundhouse-style shed less than a mile away, at Battersea Park. This shed was closed in July 1934. Electrification of the main line to Brighton in January 1933 brought about a considerable reduction in that shed's allocation. The larger engines had already been transferred away, and the remaining 46 locomotives were moved to the ex-SECR shed. Electrification of the ex-LBSC lines continued, including those to Eastbourne, Hastings and Portsmouth. The Oxted lines remained steam-worked, but were mostly worked by engines from coastal or country sheds. The addition of these engines to the shed allocation brought it to an all-time high of 164 locomotives. Remarkably, at around the same time, the shed changed its identity and became known by the more familiar name of Stewarts Lane, rather than Longhedge. In preparation for this influx of engines, several improvements were carried out. A new mechanical coaling plant was provided, the shed roof was renewed, and some changes were made to improve the layout.

With the outbreak of war and the inevitable suspension of the continental services other than troop trains, the 'Lord Nelsons' left Stewarts Lane, never to return, as it turned out. After a few months of the so-called 'phoney war', the grim reality became evident with the evacuation of Dunkirk, in which the ports of Dover, Folkestone and Ramsgate played a major part. The Southern Railway's contribution to this was enormous. Aerial bombardment caused some damage to the Longhedge Works buildings, but, unlike the nearby Nine Elms depot, the running shed escaped unscathed.

After the war it was some time before the prestige services were resumed, the 'Golden Arrow' recommencing in April 1946 and the 'Night Ferry' in December 1947. At the beginning of 1946 there was an allocation of 126 locomotives, of which only 12 might be considered as one-time Battersea Park residents. In February 1946 Ramsgate shed acquired the first batch of Bulleid light Pacifics to see service on the ex-SECR lines, and, with the return of the 'Golden Arrow', members of the class began to make their appearance at Stewarts Lane. In 1950 they were joined by four new 'Merchant Navy' 4-6-2s. Initially the Bulleid light Pacific allocation was 21C133-140, all in the 'West Country' series, but as new construction continued these were later exchanged for engines with more appropriate 'Battle of Britain' names. However, by the time that all 110 light Pacifics were completed, Stewarts Lane had some of the last members of the class, 34091/2, 34100-4 with 'West Country' names.

The next development was the substantial rebuilding by BR of all 30 of the 'Merchant Navy' class and 60 of the light Pacifics. This took place between 1956 and 1961 — rather late in the day, as withdrawal of unrebuilt engines began in 1963. In June 1959 Phase I of the Kent Coast electrification took place, covering the ex-LCDR lines to Dover and Ramsgate. Most boat-train services remained steam-hauled, even on occasions via Chatham. Stewarts Lane retained about a dozen light Pacifics and some 30 other serviceable steam engines. Two years later, Phase II of the Kent Coast electrification meant a drastic reduction. Visits in 1961/2 still found about 25 serviceable engines. In June 1962 Stewarts Lane lost its BR shed code of 73A and was given the code 75D — effectively a sub-shed of Brighton. It finally closed to steam in September 1963.

NOTE: The photographs cover solely Stewarts Lane steam on former LCDR lines. The depot's small contribution to ex-LBSC lines is not shown. Acknowledgements are due to Fred Collins, for the use of photographs by the late Kenneth Wightman, and to David Clark, for sorting them out.

Stewarts Lane Shed Allocations

14 July 1934:

'Lord Nelson' 4-6-0	850/3-5/7-9/61-5
'King Arthur' ('N15') 4-6-0	763-7/72
'U1' 2-6-0	1890, 1901-10
'T9' 4-4-0	281/2, 300/1/3/4/7/10-2/4, 704/26
'L' 4-4-0	1766-70/7/9/80
'E1' 4-4-0	1019/67, 1160/3/5/79, 1497, 1504/6/7/11
'F1' 4-4-0	1042/62/78, 1149/95, 1240
'M7' 0-4-4T	481, 1700/5/7/9
'R', 'R1' 0-4-4T	1658/61/6, 1700/5/7/9
'H' 0-4-4T	1005, 1177, 1264/6, 1312/9/21/8/9, 1503/17/33/48
'C' 0-6-0	1257, 1495/8/9, 1508/73/5/6/8-82/8/90, 1683, 1712/4/6/8/22/4
'T' 0-6-0T	1600/2-4/6-9

Total: 118 locomotives

NB: This was the week before the addition of the surviving locomotives based at Battersea Park.

20 July 1953:

'Britannia' 4-6-2	70004/14
'Merchant Navy' 4-6-2	35025-8
'Battle of Britain'/ 'West Country' 4-6-2	34066-71/87-92, 34101-4
'King Arthur' ('N15') 4-6-0	30763-74/91-5
'N' 2-6-0	31409-14, 31810-2
'U1' 2-6-0	31892/3/9, 31900-6
'Schools' ('V') 4-4-0	30915
'E1' 4-4-0	31019/67, 31504/6
'D1' 4-4-0	31743/9
'L1' 4-4-0	31758/9
'W' 2-6-4T	31912/4/5
'4MT' 2-6-4T	42089-91
'2MT' 2-6-2T	41290-2/4-6
'H' 0-4-4T	31005, 31158, 31263/5/6/9, 31319-21
'Q' 0-6-0	30541-4
'Q1' 0-6-0	33018/9/22
'C' 0-6-0	31573/5/6/8-84, 31718/9
'P' 0-6-0T	31555/7
'E2' 0-6-0T	32100-7

Total: 117 locomotives

The shed yard on 13 June 1959, which was the last Saturday of full steam working before electrification of the Chatham line to the Kent Coast. At right the two roads prepared for maintenance of diesel locomotives near completion. This rebuilding can be seen at an earlier stage on page 15. While Class C 0-6-0 No 31584 has been cleaned, its tender has escaped attention. At left No 30796 *Sir Dodinas le Savage*, a 'King Arthur' 4-6-0, which until the summer of 1958 was known as the 'Pride of Hither Green'. Although transferred to Stewarts Lane it still carried a Hither Green shed plate. *R. C. Riley*

Left: A rare and probably unique occasion. On 13 June 1958, owing to rough seas in the English Channel, No 35028 *Clan Line* was some hours late with the up 'Night Ferry', and was about to enter the shed as 'West Country' class 4-6-2 No 34092 *City of Wells* was about to leave to work the down 'Golden Arrow'. Both engines are now preserved. *R. C. Riley*

Above: Another view of *City of Wells,* on 15 June 1958, showing the coal stage and the South London line overbridge. After some years of working main-line steam charter trains, No 34092 is currently back on the Keighley & Worth Valley Railway undergoing an expensive major overhaul. *R. C. Riley*

Left: On 20 October 1957, Class H 0-4-4T No 31261 hauls the 'Golden Arrow' empty stock from the carriage sheds, while train engine No 70014 *Iron Duke* stands by in readiness to provide banking assistance on the climb to Grosvenor Bridge. Note the baggage box truck, by this time to be seen only on this service. *R. C. Riley*

Above: Passing the carriage washing plant, Wainwright Class C 0-6-0 No 31583 takes the 'Bournemouth Belle' stock out to Battersea yard, where an engine provided by Nine Elms (anything from an 0-6-0 to a 4-6-2), will haul the cars to Clapham Junction and thence Waterloo, on 10 May 1959. No 31583 was one of nine 'C' class 0-6-0s built at Longhedge Works, these being the last engines to be built there. *R. C. Riley*

Although the most appropriately-named 'Merchant Navy', No 35001 *Channel Packet* spent little time at Stewarts Lane. It was there for two weeks in April 1946 as 21C1 when it worked the inaugural postwar 'Golden Arrow', a press run on 13 April and first public run two days later. It returned to Stewarts Lane in January 1957 and stayed until June 1959, in which month electrification of the Chatham line to the Kent Coast took place. It was recorded on 10 May 1959, and was rebuilt three months later. *R. C. Riley*

At this time the now-famous survivor, No 35028 *Clan Line*, was also at Stewarts Lane in unrebuilt condition, and was recorded climbing Grosvenor Bank out of Victoria with the 11.00am Dover Continental Express on 15 September 1957. This was one of the services which included a Pullman car in its formation. *R. C. Riley*

'Merchant Navy' class 4-6-2 No 35015 *Rotterdam Lloyd* was a Stewarts Lane engine from June 1956. Rebuilt two years later, it was the only MN rebuild to appear on Eastern Section lines. It is seen approaching Factory Junction, Battersea, on 21 March 1959. At this point, its passengers could have a grandstand view of Stewarts Lane shed. No 35015 returned to Nine Elms in June 1959 and was one of the first of the class to be withdrawn, in February 1964. *R. C. Riley*

Another view of No 35015 *Rotterdam Lloyd*, in charge of the down 'Golden Arrow' leaving Penge Tunnel on 18 May 1959. From being First-class Pullmans only, the train now has First/Third-class cars, with two coaches for non-Pullman passengers.

After the 1959 electrification it continued with electric locomotive haulage, but ran for the last time on 30 September 1972. *R. C. Riley*

Left: With the introduction of the BR 'Britannia' class 4-6-2s in 1951 it was decreed that some should be seen on prestige services. Nos 70004 *William Shakespeare* and 70014 *Iron Duke* were allocated to Stewarts Lane to work the 'Golden Arrow' and other continental expresses. (Boat trains on the SR were so called when carriage roof boards were provided.) With an abundance of Bulleid Pacifics, they were not really needed, and No 70004 was exhibited at the Festival of Britain site between April and October 1951. They were transferred away to the LMR in June 1958; No 70014 was recorded on 20 October 1957. *R. C. Riley*

Above: The Bulleid light Pacifics were built between 1946 and 1951. Of these, 104 were built at Brighton Works, the remaining six at Eastleigh. The majority were named after West Country locations, but BR Nos 34049-90, 34109/10 were given names associated with the Battle of Britain. Although the latter names were more appropriate to lines in Kent, in fact the engines were allocated indiscriminately. No 34068 *Kenley* stands on shed, 10 May 1959. *R. C. Riley*

Phase II of the Kent Coast electrification, achieved in June 1961, covered the SER main line, hitherto not electrified beyond Sevenoaks. Continental expresses continued to use this route after the Chatham line electrification because the grades of the former SER line were less severe. During the last week of steam haulage, a rebuilt Bulleid light Pacific leaves Victoria with the 10.30am Dover train. *N. W. Sprinks*

16

Class H 0-4-4T No 31542 renders banking assistance at the rear of the same train.
This engine survived until November 1962. *N. W. Sprinks*

Left: Rebuilt 'Battle of Britain' class 4-6-2 No 34088 *213 Squadron* tackles the climb of Grosvenor Bank with the down 'Golden Arrow', 10 September 1960. The engine chosen for this service was normally the most recently-outshopped 4-6-2, and it was always accorded special attention by Cleaner's Chargeman Syd Norman and his gang. *R. C. Riley*

Above: Approaching Herne Hill, junction of the former LCDR West End and City lines, No 34085 *501 Squadron* heads the down 'Golden Arrow' on 10 May 1959. *R. C. Riley*

19

Above: 'King Arthur' class 4-6-0 No 30795 *Sir Dinadan* leaves Bromley South with a down Kent Coast Express on 25 May 1958. Again, the use of the word 'express' is a courtesy title, which today might be better described as a limited-stop service. This engine was one of the series built for the Brighton Section, with a six-wheeled tender, but this had been replaced two months earlier with an eight-wheeled tender from the last of the Urie 'Arthurs', No 30738 *Sir Pellinore. R. C. Riley*

Right: Passing Bickley station, No 30767 *Sir Valence* on the down 'Kentish Belle' overtakes Ashford-built 'N' class 2-6-0 No 31404 on a down excursion train, 5 August 1957. The 'Kentish Belle' ran in the summer service only, and was withdrawn following the June 1959 electrification of the former LCDR lines to the Kent Coast. *R. C. Riley*

An unidentified 'Merchant Navy' class 4-6-2 heads the up 'Night Ferry' through Shortlands. This was never an easy train to photograph because the sun was behind the train, so the best option was on a sunless day that was not too dull.

22   *K. W. Wightman*

Two unidentified 'Battle of Britain' class 4-6-2s in charge of the up 'Night Ferry',
the headcode denoting that the train had run via Chatham, hence, perhaps, the
powerful locomotive combination; it was more usual for the pilot engine to be a
4-4-0. *K. W. Wightman*

Above: The last day of the steam-hauled 'Night Ferry', when patronage was so high that the Wagons Lits trains ran in duplicate and a third train comprised the BR coaches, to be seen latterly at the country end conveying 'walk on/walk off' passengers. Passing Sydenham Hill on 13 June 1959 are Class L1 4-4-0 No 31753 and 'Battle of Britain' class 4-6-2 No 34068 *Kenley. R. C. Riley*

Right: 'Britannia' class 4-6-2 No 70004 *William Shakespeare* passes the listed waterworks building at Shortlands in charge of the down 'Golden Arrow' also with a carriage providing for non-Pullman passengers. *K. W. Wightman*

Hauling a heavy continental express through Beckenham Junction, the first Bulleid light Pacific to be rebuilt, in June 1957, was No 34005 *Barnstaple*. The badly-fixed board 'D6' on the smokebox indicates that it was bound for Dover Marine. Just behind the fourth coach can be seen Beckenham Junction signalbox, which closed in 1959. *K. W. Wightman*

In dramatic lighting conditions, then-unrebuilt 4-6-2 No 34103 *Calstock* heads an up
continental express past Shortlands Junction signalbox, which closed on 31 May
1959. It had replaced the previous SECR signalbox in 1926. *K. W. Wightman*

Below: With the chimneys of Battersea Power Station, then intact, in the background, 'Schools' class 4-4-0 No 30908 *Westminster* was in charge of a Dover boat train near Factory Junction on 23 August 1958. *R. C. Riley*

Right: In 1948 the BR Board decided that the 'Schools' class 4-4-0s were to be painted lined black. With a degree of autonomy given to the Regions in 1956, Eastleigh began, rightly, to repaint them in green upon works visits. No 30914 *Eastbourne* was one of four engines of the class not to be repainted thus, and was recorded at Stewarts Lane on 24 May 1958. *R. C. Riley*

Stewarts Lane shed had a fine reputation for cleaning engines to work special trains; after all, it had the daily job of turning out an immaculate engine for the 'Golden Arrow'. Once a year, though, it would turn out an immaculate 'Schools' class 4-4-0 to work the Royal Train to Tattenham Corner on Derby Day. This duty was performed by No 30926 *Repton* in 1961 and 1962, the latter year being the last time, as the 'Schools' class 4-4-0s were all withdrawn at the end of 1962. The last steam-hauled Derby Day Royal Train was worked by No 34088 *213 Squadron* in 1963.

Three of the 'Schools' class are preserved, and of these No 30926 *Repton* spent the years 1966-89 at Steamtown, Bellows Falls, Vermont, USA. When it was repatriated it went to the North Yorkshire Moors Railway. *D. T. Cobbe*

This relief Ramsgate train was diagrammed to work via the Catford Loop and has 'Schools' class 4-4-0 No 30936 *Cranleigh* in charge, passing Denmark Hill, 16 May 1959. This part of the line was jointly LBSCR/LCDR-owned, and the former company built a handsome station on the road overbridge. Sadly this was destroyed by arsonists in March 1980, but the determination of the Camberwell Society in obtaining grants and finding an end user resulted in the station being totally rebuilt in its original form, and a large part of it reopened four years later as 'The Phoenix and Firkin', at that time part of a chain of pubs run by Bruce's Breweries. Worth a visit! *R. C. Riley*

Left: Then still in black livery, No 30913 *Christ's Hospital* works a down Ramsgate relief train near Shortlands Junction, 2 August 1958. *R. C. Riley*

Below: Another 'Schools' class 4-4-0, No 30938 *St Olaves*, heads a relief Ramsgate express up, near Shortlands Junction. That portion of the line towards the front of the train was enlarged to four tracks in 1959. *K. W. Wightman*

Left: 'King Arthur' class 4-6-0 No 30794 *Sir Ector de Maris* is causing a degree of pollution as it heads past Downsbridge Road bridge, Shortlands, on a down Ramsgate train. While the bridge remains double-track only, the line immediately to the south of it was quadrupled in 1959. This engine, from the 793-806 batch built for service on the former LBSC main line, retained its six-wheel tender until withdrawal in 1960. These engines were so fitted to enable them to use the smaller turntables available. *K. W. Wightman*

Above: No 30804 *Sir Cador of Cornwall* leaves Bromley South on a down Ramsgate train. This engine also retained its six-wheel tender, although others were fitted with eight-wheel tenders from older 4-6-0s withdrawn from service. The LCDR signalbox closed on 31 May 1959. *K. W. Wightman*

Class D1 4-4-0 No 31749 waits outside Bromley South with a down Ramsgate excursion. The first four carriages of Set 471 are from the last train to be built at the former LBSC Lancing Works. On entry into service in 1926 it had a substantial number of First-class carriages in its formation and was used on the 'City Limited' between Brighton and London Bridge. It lost these coaches following electrification of the Brighton main line in 1933, when it went into general service. Some features of the coaches, notably the bogies, relate to the 'Ironclad' stock of the LSWR.

K. W. Wightman

A few minutes later, another of the 'Brighton Arthur' series, No 30796 *Sir Dodinas le Savage,* passes the stock of the excursion on the down main line. *K. W. Wightman*

Left: The restricted layout at Charing Cross caused the SECR to divert all its continental traffic to Victoria after World War 1. At that time the bridges on former LCDR lines were unable to take the load of heavy locomotives — even the 'L' class 4-4-0s were not permitted. Something had to be done urgently, and in 1919 Class E 4-4-0 No 179 was rebuilt at Ashford, superheated with 10in-piston valves and thoroughly modernised. This resulted in a very successful engine, and 10 more were so rebuilt, together with 21 Class D engines. Class D1 4-4-0 No 31749 stands at Stewarts Lane on 24 May 1958. *R. C. Riley*

Above: By 1925, bridge-strengthening on the LCDR line enabled the use of larger locomotives, but, right up to the 1959 Kent Coast electrification, these lively 4-4-0s were still to be seen on relief trains with eight or nine coaches. Class D1 4-4-0 No 31749 heads an up train near Factory Junction, its passengers having a good view of Stewarts Lane shed, on 25 June 1958. *R. C. Riley*

Left: Class E1 4-4-0 No 31507 in charge of an up Ramsgate van train near Shortlands Junction. The rebuilds looked very similar. The 'E1s' had a longer wheelbase and fluted coupling rods, which provided a means of identification. *K. W. Wightman*

Below: The same train at the same location, with Class D1 4-4-0 No 31741 at the head. Note that in both views the track widening had been carried out. *K. W. Wightman*

Left: No 31810, as SECR No 810, was the pioneer Maunsell Mogul of the 'N' class, having emerged from Ashford Works in August 1917. With the problems of the war it was 1920 before further members of the class appeared. The design was chosen as a project for construction at Woolwich Arsenal to help maintain employment after the war, the boilers being supplied by normal railway contractors. Lack of expertise caused the 50 engines ordered by the SECR to be delivered as kits of parts to be assembled at Ashford in 1924/5. These were very useful engines and were to be found throughout the SR system. There were eventually 80 members of the class. Similar engines emerging from the Woolwich order were to be found on the Great Southern Railway, Ireland, and in tank-engine form on the Metropolitan Railway.

In these photographs No 31810 had become derailed at Shortlands Junction on the up Ramsgate van train on 11 April 1958. The cause is not known, but track widening was taking place at the time. The new signalbox was under construction, and came into use on 31 May 1959. *Both: K. W. Wightman*

Above: A member of the last batch of 'N' class 2-6-0s to be built, in 1932, No 31404 heads an up Ramsgate train near Shortlands Junction on 2 August 1958. At that time, this was the August Bank Holiday weekend and 'N' class 2-6-0s, together with the remarkable 'D1'/'E1' 4-4-0s, could be found substituting for larger engines. *R. C. Riley*

43

At the same time that No 810 left Ashford, a very similar 2-6-4T appeared —
No 790 — with 6ft 3in driving wheels against the 5ft 6in of the 'N' class. In SR days
the 20 engines of the class were named after rivers. In August 1927, after a period of
heavy rain, No A800 *River Cray* was involved in a serious derailment at Riverhead,
near Sevenoaks. The condition of the track was mainly to blame, but the engines
were withdrawn and rebuilt as 2-6-0 tender engines, known as the 'U' class. These
engines were not normally to be found on ex-SECR lines, but the three-cylinder
version, Class U1, found regular employment in the area. The first, No A890, had
been part of the ill-fated 'River' class but emerged as a tender engine in 1928, 20
more such engines being built in 1931. No 31892 was recorded on a down Ramsgate
express passing Ravensbourne on the Catford Loop line. *K. W. Wightman*

Stewarts Lane enginemen referred to these engines as 'U-Boats'. No 31897 heads an up Ramsgate express at St Mary Cray Junction on 16 May 1959. Forty years later, with the proliferation of package holidays abroad and motor-car usage, it is hard to recall that the Kent Coast resorts were so popular and that every Saturday in the summer they required an intensive train service. *R. C. Riley*

Left: Also near St Mary Cray on 16 May 1959, No 31876 heads an up Ramsgate express, this engine being one of six engines of Class N1, a three-cylinder version of the 'N' class. Note the track widening taking place in readiness for the June 1959 electrification. The Maunsell Mogul variants numbered 157 at their peak. The three-cylinder engines were withdrawn in 1962, but some members of Classes N and U survived another four years. *R. C. Riley*

Above: The 15 members of the 'W' class built between 1932 and 1936 were effectively tank versions of the 'N1' class. They were intended to be used for transfer freight trains to the LMS at Brent and Willesden and the GWR at Old Oak Common. With their 5ft 6in wheels they could work the loose-coupled freight trains at a reasonable speed to keep out of the way of the suburban electric trains. Having regard to the tragic Sevenoaks accident, they were not allowed to work passenger trains. 2-6-4T No 31914 was recorded at Stewarts Lane on 10 May 1959. *R. C. Riley*

47

Below: In 1955 10 BR Standard Class 5 4-6-0s — Nos 73080-9 — were allocated to Stewarts Lane, of a batch built at Derby. In the same year 12 Class 4 4-6-0s of Swindon build also appeared. Some were initially allocated to Dover, but it was not until 1962 that they were shedded at Stewarts Lane, when they were equally at home on former LBSC lines. No 73085 was recorded on an up Ramsgate express near St Mary Cray Junction on 11 May 1957. *R. C. Riley*

Right: Before the 1959 electrification of the former LCDR main line several track improvements were carried out, and this view shows No 73083 on an up Ramsgate express at the same location two years later, on 18 May 1959. *R. C. Riley*

Left: St Mary Cray station had been one of those often favoured by the SECR companies, having staggered platforms. With the 1959 track widening the opportunity was taken to build a new station. No 73041 was passing the new station on an up empty stock train on 16 May 1959. When the two 'Britannias' were transferred to the LMR in June 1958, Nos 73041/2 took their place at Stewarts Lane. *R. C. Riley*

Above: Class 5 4-6-0 No 73041 heads a down Dover boat train approaching Bickley on 13 June 1959, the day before Phase I of the Kent Coast electrification. In the sidings the new '4-CEP' electric units await entry into traffic. *R. C. Riley*

Left: Wainwright Class C 0-6-0 No 31575 heads a train of empty milk tanks to Kensington past Stewarts Lane, 30 August 1958. There were 109 of these sturdy engines, of which nine were built at Longhedge Works — the last to be assembled there. These engines proved their worth in hauling the greatly-increased freight traffic to the Channel Ports in World War 1. One of these engines — No 31592, built at Longhedge Works — survives on the Bluebell Railway. *R. C. Riley*

Above: Latterly Stewarts Lane had two re-boilered Stirling 0-6-0s of Class O1 on its allocation. These were used on freight and milk trains, an occasional ECS train and even enthusiasts' specials. No 31370 was recorded on 1 March 1959; following electrification, this locomotive lasted until February 1960, its partner, No 31048, remaining in service at Dover until October 1960. No 31065 survives on the Bluebell Railway. *R. C. Riley*

53

The Pullman cars for the 'Bournemouth Belle' were maintained in the carriage sheds at Stewarts Lane. Each day they were hauled to Clapham Junction, where they reversed to work into Waterloo, with a similar operation each evening. Nine Elms supplied the motive power, normally a tender engine — anything from an 0-6-0 to a 4-6-2. On 10 May 1959 Class Q1 0-6-0 No 33038 was in charge. This provides a good view of the coaling plant. *R. C. Riley*

The spur line carrying traffic from Clapham Junction or the West London line passed over the back of Stewarts Lane shed, joining the main line at Factory Junction, where Class Q1 0-6-0 No 33027 was stopped by signals on 30 August 1958. It was in charge of a transfer freight from Feltham to Hither Green. *R. C. Riley*

Recently ex works, an immaculate 'H' class 0-4-4T heads the empty Pullman cars to Victoria for the 'Kentish Belle', 15 September 1957. Note the sharp grade out of the terminus up Grosvenor Bank. This train started life in the summer of 1948 as the 'Thanet Belle', but was changed in 1951 at the time of a short-lived service of part of the train to Canterbury, which lasted only two years. This train ran only during the summer service. *R. C. Riley*.

There were 66 of the useful 'H' class 0-4-4Ts. With the withdrawal of ex-LBSC 'D3' and SECR 'R'/'R1' 0-4-4Ts, many of the class were equipped for pull-and-push working. No 31551 was recorded at Stewarts Lane on 24 May 1958, and was motor-fitted two years later. *R. C. Riley*

Below: When the disadvantages of the steam railcars became apparent, construction of eight small 0-6-0Ts forming the 'P' class was authorised in 1909/10. They were to be fitted for pull-and-push working, for which they were adequate on lightly-loaded branch trains. By 1924, in SR days, all were concentrated at Dover and Folkestone, where their short wheelbase was suitable for harbour lines. Stewarts Lane had a sharply-curved siding to the CWS milk depot. This saw a great variety of small locomotives, but eventually the 'P' class became the favoured type. Behind No 31558 on 20 October 1957 can be seen part of the Longhedge Works. This engine was scrapped in 1960, but four of the class survive on the Bluebell and Kent & East Sussex railways, where they have proved popular engines. *R. C. Riley*

Right: Ten LMR Ivatt Class 2 2-6-2Ts, Nos 41290-9, were allocated to the SR in 1951, later to be joined by 20 more, and these proved very successful replacing older pre-Grouping types. They were widely allocated throughout the SR and, as steam became displaced elsewhere, some older members of the class came to the SR. On 20 October 1957 No 41291, also beside the Longhedge Works building, was about to haul the 'Bournemouth Belle' ECS from the carriage sheds to enable 'U' class 2-6-0 No 31621 to be coupled on to take the stock to Clapham Junction. *R. C. Riley*

Above: Class L 4-4-0 No 31775 was one of 10 of the class built by A. Borsig, Berlin, and delivered by July 1914 — just before the outbreak of war. Beyer, Peacock built a further 12, but in SECR days they were too heavy for LCDR lines and this continued to be the case even in early SR days. In the last years, Faversham and Ramsgate had a small allocation, and they appeared occasionally at Victoria. Ashford-based No 31775 was recorded passing Downsbridge Road Bridge at Shortlands with a down Ramsgate train. *K. W. Wightman*

Right: When in 1922 the SECR introduced non-stop expresses between Charing Cross and Folkestone Central, it was found that the 'L' class could not maintain the schedules. A Class D1 was tried and found successful, but at the time none could be spared from their work on former LCDR lines. Hence a redesigned version of the 'L' class was ordered: 15 engines of Class L1 built by the North British Locomotive Co in 1926. Dover-based No 31754, fresh from its last general overhaul, stands on Stewarts Lane shed on 15 June 1958. *R. C. Riley*

Left: Class D1 4-4-0 No 31545 heads an up Ramsgate train of nine-coach length past the 1926 signalbox at Shortlands Junction, on August Bank Holiday Saturday (2 August) 1958. The later batch of Bulleid light Pacifics had an active life of 15 years; No 31545 lasted 15 years in original condition and a further 40 years in rebuilt form — the record of the 'D1'/'E1' 4-4-0s is quite remarkable. Their longevity owed much to the fact that they were the heaviest engines allowed into Holborn Viaduct, then a busy centre for parcels traffic. *R. C. Riley*

Below: Also at Shortlands Junction on 2 August 1958, No 34092 *City of Wells* heads an up 'Continental Express' with the standard load of 12 bogies and two vans. However, this was one of the more important such trains, since it includes two Pullman cars in its formation. This view gives a good impression of the widening that had taken place, although the new tracks were not then in use. *R. C. Riley*

Left: An unidentified 'Schools' class 4-4-0 heads a shorter-formation boat train relief at Shortlands. *K. W. Wightman*

Above: 'Schools' class 4-4-0 No 30937 *Epsom* in charge of a down Kent express at St Mary Cray Junction on Whit Monday, 16 May 1959. Here also, the quadrupling is virtually complete but not in use. *R. C. Riley*

Below: On the Chatham route, No 34101 *Hartland* tackles the climb of Sole Street Bank with an up Dover Continental Express. Stewarts Lane tried to keep its more important locomotives clean but this one has escaped the cleaner's attention. One of the six Bulleid light Pacifics to be built at Eastleigh, No 34101 was rebuilt in 1960 and survives in preservation. *K. W. Wightman*

Right: Also tackling the five-mile climb of 1 in 100 of Sole Street Bank, No 30796 *Sir Dodinas le Savage* was recorded with an up Ramsgate express. One of two 'King Arthurs' shedded at Hither Green with the 5.47pm Cannon Street-Dover included in its duty, this engine was normally immaculate. However, with the delivery of new 'Hastings' diesel units, this train was dieselised in June 1958, thereby explaining the engine's later lacklustre condition. *K. W. Wightman*

Ramsgate shed had the services of elderly Stirling 'O' class 0-6-0 No A98 to provide carriage heating from 1929 to 1953. In the latter year it was replaced by No 31501, one of the handsome 'D' class 4-4-0s of which No 737 is preserved at the National Railway Museum. No 31501 stands beside 'King Arthur' class 4-4-0 No 30793 *Sir Ontzlake* on 28 March 1959. *R. C. Riley*

Just over a year later, on 14 May 1960, No 31501 is dwarfed by the erection of a new carriage shed for electric multiple-units in readiness for Phase II of the Kent Coast electrification. *R. C. Riley*

Left: Also at Ramsgate shed on 14 May 1960 was Class D1 4-4-0 No 31743 of Stewarts Lane. Note that these popular little engines were kept in clean condition. *R. C. Riley*

Above: Bricklayers Arms-based Class D1 4-4-0 No 31735 receives the attention of the ash-disposal man at Ramsgate shed, 23 May 1959. The engine is quite clean, but not up to Stewarts Lane standard! *R. C. Riley*

Below: Also from Bricklayers Arms shed, Class E1 4-4-0 No 31507 heads a Sheerness-Charing Cross train on 14 June 1958. The St Mary Cray Junction signalbox in the background had less than a year's operational service left. *R. C. Riley*

Right: A sad occasion. In clean condition, the last 'D1', No 31749, pilots the last 'E1', No 31067, on an Engineer's Department train at Sevenoaks Bat & Ball, 4 November 1961. The two engines were making their way to Ashford Works to be broken up. *R. C. Riley*

Left: One of the sturdy Wainwright Class C 0-6-0s, No 31256 shunts the yard at Faversham on 30 September 1958. This was and remains an important junction on the Kent Coast line, at which the Dover and Ramsgate lines diverge. *R. C. Riley*

Above: Passing the 1926 shed at Ramsgate, Class C 0-6-0 No 31245 hauls an empty-stock train into the yards for the cleaner's attention on 28 March 1959. This 1902-built engine was to survive only two months after the June 1959 electrification. Nevertheless, it had run 1,390,045 miles in the course of its 57-year career. *R. C. Riley*

Left: Maunsell 'N' class Mogul No 31861 heads out of Margate on an Ashford train on 28 March 1959. It was withdrawn four years later, the last survivors going in 1966. *R. C. Riley*

Above: A comparatively rare visitor to Stewarts Lane, on 2 April 1960, was this ex-LBSCR 'K' class 2-6-0, No 32352. Not seen on passenger trains as often as their SECR counterparts, they were nevertheless very strong engines. Bert Wood, Mechanical Foreman at this time, said that if a Class K had a rough shunt with a Maunsell Mogul, the latter would need to go to works, the LBSC engine having a bufferbeam one inch thicker! An exaggeration, maybe, since his own fitters could probably have dealt with it, but was praise indeed for a good Brighton engine from a dedicated Chatham man. *R. C. Riley*

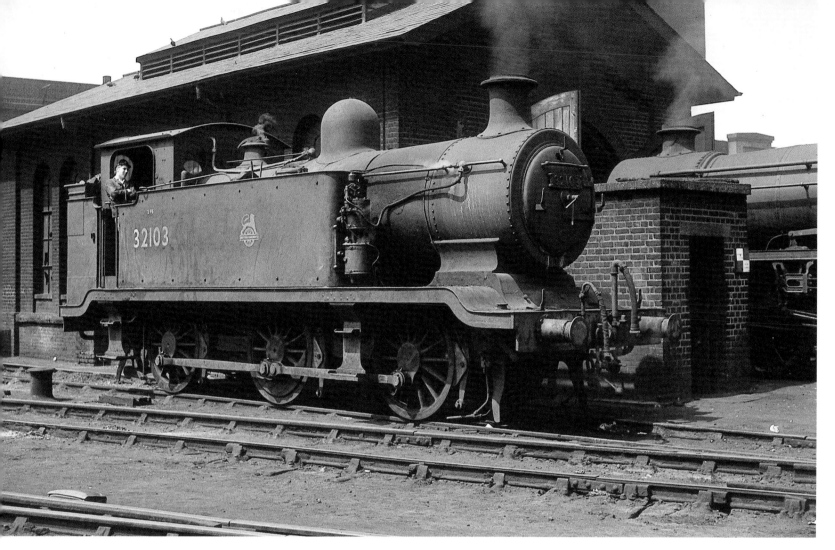

Above: A last tenuous link with the LCDR remained until 1936, when five of the 10 'T' class 0-6-0Ts were withdrawn, leaving two survivors at Stewarts Lane. Replacement came in the form of ex-LBSCR Class E2 0-6-0Ts, some of which were already on the allocation following the closure of Battersea Park shed in 1934. No 32103 stands outside the weighbridge, something of a luxury at a running shed and probably related to the presence of Longhedge Works. The 'E2s' were used to shunt Herne Hill Sorting Sidings and to work empty-stock trains to and from Victoria. *R. C. Riley*

Right: The imposing building at Dover Marine came into use towards the end of World War 1 but was not formally opened to the public until 1919. Class O1 0-6-0 No 31434 stands beside the station while engaged in van shunting. In more recent years the station became known as Dover Western Docks, until its closure following the opening of the Channel Tunnel. It is a listed structure and contains the elaborate SECR War Memorial, but it now serves as a cruise-liner terminal. *R. C. Riley*